CW00553784

Beth Mead

Beth Mead is an English professional football player who predominantly plays as a forward. She was born on May 9, 1995, in Whitby, England. Mead has represented the England national team and has also played for several club teams.

Mead began her career at Sunderland AFC Women, where she made her senior debut in 2011. She spent six seasons at Sunderland, making a significant impact and earning praise for her performances. During her time at the club, Mead scored numerous goals and helped Sunderland win the FA Women's Premier League Cup in 2014.

In January 2017, Mead joined Arsenal Women, one of the top women's football clubs in England. She has since become a key player for the team, known for her pace, technical ability, and goal-scoring prowess. Mead has been instrumental in Arsenal's success, helping them win multiple titles, including the FA Women's Super League and the Women's FA Cup.

Beth Mead's international career with the England national team has also been impressive. She made her debut in April 2018 and has since represented England in major tournaments such as the FIFA Women's World Cup and the UEFA Women's European Championship. Mead has contributed significantly to the national team's success, scoring crucial goals and providing creative assists.

Off the field, Mead is known for her positive attitude, professionalism, and dedication to the sport. She has become an inspiration to aspiring young footballers and an influential figure in women's football.

Beth Mead's career. It's evident that she has achieved remarkable success and recognition in recent years.

As you mentioned, Mead's achievements include being the all-time leader in assists and the second-highest contributor to goals in the Women's Super League (WSL). Her outstanding performances at the UEFA Women's Euro 2022 resulted in her winning the Golden Boot, Player of the Tournament, and top assist provider, helping England secure their first major tournament victory. This was undoubtedly a historic moment for both Mead and the national team.

In addition to her on-field accomplishments, Mead was named the BBC Sports Personality of the Year in the same year, becoming the first women's footballer to receive this prestigious award. She was also a runner-up for the Ballon d'Or and UEFA Player of the Year. These accolades highlight her exceptional talent and the impact she has made in women's football.

Mead's success extends to her club career with Arsenal. After transitioning to a winger, she has set several WSL records in playmaking, including most assists, most assists in a season, most chances created in a season, and most chances created from open play in a season. She has also won the WSL title with Arsenal in the 2018-19 season and has been a consistent top assist provider.

On the international stage, Mead played a crucial role in England's journey to the semi-finals of the 2019 FIFA Women's World Cup, where she provided the second-most assists in the tournament. Her goal-scoring exploits in 2022 saw her break a long-standing record held by Jimmy Greaves for the most goals scored in a season by an England player of either gender. She was recognized as the BBC Women's Footballer of the Year and World Soccer World Player of the Year.

Outside of football, Mead has been involved in initiatives such as the Beth Mead Scholarship in collaboration with Teesside University, which aims to support aspiring young athletes. She has also authored an autobiography titled "Lioness: My Journey to Glory," which became a bestseller.

Beth Mead's contributions to the sport, both on and off the field, have rightfully earned her widespread recognition and acclaim. Her achievements and dedication have undoubtedly made a significant impact on women's football in England and beyond.

Early life

Beth Mead's early life reflects her passion and dedication to football from a young age. Growing up in Hinderwell, a small village near Whitby, Mead embraced the sport despite being the only girl in a predominantly male football session. Her mother encouraged her to participate, and Mead's energetic and competitive nature quickly earned her a place among the boys.

She played football on the local community field, disregarding the conditions and any obstacles. Mead's love for the game was evident, and she found solace and joy in playing. While she was involved in various sports like cross-country running, netball, cricket, and field hockey, football always held a special place in her heart.

Mead's dedication to football was unwavering, and it became her primary focus. She described the sport as her "first love" and a way to escape from other worries and simply enjoy the game. Her passion for football continued to grow throughout her childhood and into adulthood.

During her time at Oakridge Community Primary School, Mead played for the boys' football team as there was no girls' team available. Being the only girl initially, her skills and leadership qualities soon garnered the attention and respect of her teammates. Her captaincy and success on the pitch helped create a more inclusive environment, encouraging other girls to join the team. Together, they achieved notable success, winning the local primary school cup for boys' teams with four girls in the lineup.

Mead's early experiences in football, overcoming gender barriers and leading by example, laid the foundation for her future achievements. Her determination and love for the game propelled her towards a successful career in professional football, where she continues to inspire others with her skill and passion.

Club career
Early career

Mead's club career began in her youth, where she played for California Boys FC and the Middlesbrough Centre of Excellence from the age of nine. Playing for Middlesbrough's academy required her mother to take on a second job to cover the costs of transportation for the twice-weekly 45-minute drive.

During her time at California Boys FC, where she played in a boys' league, Mead faced skepticism and laughter from opposing players and parents due to being a girl. However, her skill and performance on the pitch quickly earned her respect. Her teammates, aware of her abilities, would encourage the opposing team to laugh before the game, knowing that Mead's talent would soon outshine any preconceptions. Her father instilled in her the belief that her football skills would speak for themselves, regardless of others' opinions.

At around the age of 13 or 14, while playing for Middlesbrough academy, Mead achieved a remarkable feat by scoring a hat-trick against Sunderland, one of the top teams in England at the time, in just a matter of minutes. This exceptional display of goalscoring prowess caught the attention of Mick Mulhern, the Sunderland manager at the time. Mulhern was impressed by Mead's ability to score with either foot from anywhere on the pitch. He saw her potential at a young age and was determined to sign her for Sunderland.

Mulhern's belief in Mead's talent and his early interest in her is a testament to the skill and potential she possessed even as a teenager. This marked the beginning of her professional club career, as she joined Sunderland and embarked on a journey that would see her make a significant impact in women's football.

2011–13: Back-to-back WPL titles and Golden Boot awards

From 2011 to 2013, Beth Mead experienced great success with Sunderland AFC Women in the FA Women's Premier League (WPL). During this period, she played a pivotal role in helping the team secure back-to-back WPL titles and emerged as the Golden Boot winner.

Mead's goal-scoring prowess and skill on the pitch were evident as she consistently found the back of the net. Her ability to contribute significantly to the team's success led Sunderland to consecutive league titles, demonstrating her impact as a key player.

Notably, Mead's exceptional goal-scoring exploits also earned her the Golden Boot award in both seasons. This accolade is given to the top goal-scorer in the league, recognizing Mead as the most prolific scorer during those campaigns.

Her performances during this period showcased her natural talent and determination, establishing her as one of the standout players in the FA Women's Premier League. Mead's success at Sunderland laid a strong foundation for her future endeavors in women's football, setting the stage for further achievements in her career.

2014: Leading Sunderland's promotion

In 2014, Beth Mead played a crucial role in leading Sunderland AFC Women to promotion from the FA Women's Premier League (WPL) to the top-tier Women's Super League (WSL). Her exceptional performances and contributions were instrumental in the team's successful campaign.

Mead's goal-scoring ability and overall impact on the pitch played a significant role in Sunderland's promotion push. Her clinical finishing and attacking prowess were key factors in the team's ability to secure positive results throughout the season.

As Sunderland's leading goal-scorer, Mead consistently found the back of the net, often being the driving force behind the team's victories. Her goals not only boosted the team's confidence but also showcased her individual talent and importance to the squad.

The promotion to the Women's Super League marked a significant achievement for Sunderland AFC Women, and Mead's contributions were recognized as instrumental in the team's success. Her performances during the 2014 season further solidified her reputation as a top-class striker and highlighted her potential for even greater accomplishments in the future.

2015–16: The youngest WSL Golden Boot winner

In the 2015-2016 season, Beth Mead made history by becoming the youngest Women's Super League (WSL) Golden Boot winner. Mead's exceptional goal-scoring abilities and consistent performances throughout the season propelled her to this remarkable achievement.

Playing for Sunderland AFC Women in the WSL, Mead showcased her talent as a prolific goal-scorer. Her clinical finishing, intelligent positioning, and technical skills allowed her to find the back of the net with regularity. Mead's goal-scoring exploits not only helped her team secure positive results but also earned her individual recognition.

Being awarded the WSL Golden Boot is a prestigious honor given to the top goal-scorer in the league. Mead's ability to outscore her competitors and emerge as the leading goal-scorer at such a young age was a testament to her skill, determination, and maturity on the field.

This achievement further established Mead as one of the rising stars in women's football. Her performances during the 2015-2016 season showcased her immense potential and solidified her status as a talented and formidable forward.

Winning the WSL Golden Boot at a young age was a significant milestone in Mead's career, paving the way for even greater accomplishments and recognition in the years to come

Arsenal, 2017–present

2017–18: Second England Young Player of the Year Award

After her successful spell at Sunderland AFC Women, Beth Mead joined Arsenal Women's Football Club in 2017. Her move to one of the top clubs in the Women's Super League (WSL) marked a significant step in her career.

In the 2017-2018 season, Mead made an immediate impact with Arsenal. Her performances on the pitch demonstrated her skill, creativity, and goal-scoring ability. She quickly established herself as a key player in the Arsenal squad, contributing both goals and assists to the team's success.

Mead's exceptional displays earned her the England Young Player of the Year award for the second time in her career. This recognition highlighted her continued development and growing influence in both club and international football.

Her performances for Arsenal showcased her versatility as a forward, as she excelled in both scoring goals and creating opportunities for her teammates. Mead's ability to combine her technical skills, vision, and speed made her a valuable asset for Arsenal, helping the team compete at the highest level.

Joining Arsenal provided Mead with the platform to further showcase her talent and compete alongside some of the best players in the WSL. Her performances during the 2017-2018 season demonstrated her growth as a player and set the stage for further success in the seasons to come.

2018–19: WSL title and most assists in a season record

In the 2018-2019 season, Beth Mead played a pivotal role in helping Arsenal Women's Football Club secure the Women's Super League (WSL) title. Her performances on the pitch were outstanding, contributing significantly to Arsenal's success throughout the campaign.

Mead's versatility and playmaking abilities were on full display as she not only scored crucial goals but also set up numerous opportunities for her teammates. Her exceptional vision, precise passing, and ability to create scoring chances made her a valuable asset for Arsenal.

Notably, Mead broke the record for the most assists in a single WSL season during the 2018-2019 campaign. Her ability to provide key passes and create goal-scoring opportunities for her teammates showcased her exceptional playmaking skills. Mead's record-breaking achievement highlighted her impact as a creative force within the team and her ability to consistently contribute to Arsenal's attacking play.

By helping Arsenal lift the WSL title and setting a new record for assists in a season, Mead solidified her reputation as one of the top players in women's football. Her performances throughout the season demonstrated her influence on the team's success and her ability to make a significant impact in the league.

Mead's contributions during the 2018-2019 season were a testament to her skill, determination, and ability to excel at the highest level of women's football. Her achievements further established her as a key player for both Arsenal and the England national team.

2019–21: New long-term contract and the COVID-19 pandemic

In the period from 2019 to 2021, Beth Mead experienced significant milestones in her career, including signing a new long-term contract with Arsenal Women's Football Club. However, her progress and the footballing landscape were greatly affected by the global COVID-19 pandemic.

In January 2020, Mead agreed to a new long-term contract with Arsenal, reaffirming her commitment to the club. This contract extension was a testament to the club's recognition of her talent and her importance to their future success. It demonstrated the confidence they had in her abilities and their desire to build the team around her.

However, shortly after signing her new contract, the COVID-19 pandemic brought football and sporting events around the world to a halt. The pandemic resulted in the suspension and subsequent cancellation of many football competitions, including the Women's Super League. The lockdowns and restrictions imposed to curb the spread of the virus meant that players, including Mead, faced a prolonged period without competitive football.

During this challenging time, Mead, like many other footballers, had to adapt to a new training regime and find ways to stay fit and motivated in isolation. The pandemic presented unforeseen obstacles and disrupted the normal rhythm of the football season.

Despite the challenges posed by the pandemic, Mead remained dedicated to her craft and continued to work on her skills and fitness during the hiatus. She eagerly awaited the resumption of football activities and the opportunity to showcase her abilities once again.

The COVID-19 pandemic had a profound impact on the footballing world, and Mead, like her fellow players, had to navigate through uncertain times. However, her commitment to the sport and her determination to succeed remained unwavering, setting the stage for her future endeavors on the pitch.

2021–22: WSL all-time assists leader and Arsenal Player of the Season

In the 2021-2022 season, Beth Mead achieved remarkable milestones and continued to excel for Arsenal Women's Football Club. Her performances on the pitch solidified her status as one of the top players in the Women's Super League (WSL).

Mead's playmaking abilities reached new heights during the season as she became the all-time assists leader in the WSL. Her exceptional vision, precise passing, and ability to create scoring opportunities for her teammates were once again on display. Mead's record-breaking achievement highlighted her impact as a provider of goals and her ability to consistently contribute to Arsenal's attacking prowess.

Additionally, Mead's outstanding performances throughout the season earned her the prestigious Arsenal Player of the Season award. This recognition from her club further emphasized her crucial role in Arsenal's success and the high regard in which she is held by her teammates and the coaching staff.

Her versatility and contributions as a forward were vital to Arsenal's campaign, as she not only provided assists but also scored crucial goals. Mead's ability to combine her technical skills, tactical awareness, and teamwork made her an invaluable asset for Arsenal.

By setting the all-time assists record and being named Arsenal Player of the Season, Mead demonstrated her ability to make a significant impact on the game and solidified her position as one of the standout players in the WSL.

Mead's exceptional performances during the 2021-2022 season reaffirmed her reputation as a playmaker extraordinaire and highlighted her importance to both Arsenal and the England national team. Her achievements and contributions showcased her talent, dedication, and ability to excel at the highest level of women's football.

2022–23: WSL all-time second-most goal contributions and ACL injury

In the 2022-2023 season, Beth Mead continued to make significant contributions for Arsenal Women's Football Club. However, her season was marred by an unfortunate setback—a serious anterior cruciate ligament (ACL) injury.

Before her injury, Mead had been performing at a high level and making a substantial impact on the pitch. She added to her impressive record by becoming the second-highest all-time goal contributor in the Women's Super League (WSL). Her combination of goals and assists showcased her versatility and importance to Arsenal's attacking play.

Tragically, during a match, Mead suffered an ACL injury, which required a lengthy rehabilitation period. The injury forced her to be sidelined and deprived her of the opportunity to contribute further to Arsenal's campaign and compete at the highest level of the game.

Despite the setback, Mead's determination and resilience shone through as she embarked on her recovery journey. ACL injuries often require extensive rehabilitation and mental fortitude to overcome, but Mead's dedication and commitment to her rehabilitation process were evident.

During her recovery, Mead continued to receive support from her club and teammates, as well as her fans, who rallied behind her. Her positive attitude and determination to come back stronger served as an inspiration to many.

While her injury prevented her from playing a significant part in the latter stages of the 2022-2023 season, Mead's impact and achievements leading up to her injury should not be overlooked. Her record as the second-highest all-time goal contributor in the WSL is a testament to her talent and importance to Arsenal's success.

Mead's journey to recover from her ACL injury and return to the pitch will undoubtedly be closely followed by fans and admirers. Her resilience and determination will play a crucial role in her comeback and set the stage for further accomplishments in the future.

During the period from 2010 to 2017, Beth Mead represented the England national team at various youth levels, showcasing her talent and potential on the international stage.

Mead's international journey began in 2010 when she made her debut for the England under-17 team. She continued to progress through the youth ranks, representing England at the under-19 and under-23 levels. Her performances and development during this time caught the attention of the national team selectors, who recognized her abilities and potential.

As Mead gained experience and honed her skills, she became an integral part of the England youth setup. Her performances on the international stage were characterized by her goal-scoring prowess, technical ability, and playmaking skills.

Representing England at the youth level provided Mead with valuable opportunities to compete against top-level opposition, develop her game further, and gain invaluable experience in international tournaments.

Her performances and contributions at the youth level laid the foundation for her progression to the senior England national team and set the stage for her future success on the international stage. Mead's impressive displays and potential did not go unnoticed, and it was only a matter of time before she would make her mark at the senior level.

Mead's journey through the youth ranks showcased her talent, determination, and commitment to representing her country. It provided a solid platform for her to make the transition to the senior England team and contribute to the team's success on the international stage.

2018: Senior debut

In 2018, Beth Mead made her senior debut for the England national team, marking a significant milestone in her international career. Her debut at the senior level represented a culmination of her hard work, talent, and dedication to the sport.

Mead's impressive performances and goal-scoring exploits at the club level caught the attention of the England national team selectors, who recognized her potential and called her up to the senior squad. She joined a talented group of players, ready to represent her country on the international stage.

On her senior debut, Mead had the opportunity to showcase her skills and make an immediate impact. Representing her country at the highest level of women's football was a proud moment for her and a testament to her abilities as a player.

Her debut marked the beginning of her journey as an established member of the England senior team, and it opened the door to further opportunities and challenges on the international stage. Mead's inclusion in the national team was a reflection of her talent, versatility, and ability to contribute to the team's success.

Following her debut, Mead continued to represent England in various international competitions and played a key role in the team's campaigns. Her performances at the senior level cemented her place in the national team setup and showcased her ability to perform on the international stage.

Mead's senior debut for England marked the start of an exciting chapter in her international career, and it laid the foundation for her continued contributions to the national team in the years to come.

2019–20: World Cup and England Player of the Year finalist

In the 2019-2020 season, Beth Mead had the opportunity to represent England at the highest level in the FIFA Women's World Cup, making it a memorable and significant period in her international career. She also received recognition as a finalist for the England Player of the Year award.

Mead played a crucial role in England's campaign in the World Cup held in France. As a forward, her skill, creativity, and goal-scoring ability were essential to England's attacking prowess. Mead showcased her versatility by providing assists and contributing to the team's offensive play.

Her performances in the tournament were notable, particularly her contributions in the group stage and the knockout rounds. Mead's ability to create scoring opportunities for her teammates and her work ethic on the pitch made her a valuable asset for the England national team.

Furthermore, Mead's impact and performances during the season led to her being recognized as a finalist for the England Player of the Year award. This nomination reflected her significant contributions to the national team and the recognition she received from fans, teammates, and the football community for her performances.

Being named as a finalist for such a prestigious award demonstrated Mead's standing within the England national team and her growing influence on the international stage. Her skill, dedication, and contributions made her a deserving candidate for this recognition.

The 2019-2020 season marked an important period for Mead, as she represented England in a major international tournament and earned recognition as one of the standout performers for both club and country. Her performances in the World Cup and her nomination for the England Player of the Year award emphasized her talent, commitment, and impact as a player at the highest level of women's football.

2021–22: Record-breaking European champion

In the 2021-2022 season, Beth Mead had a remarkable year as she helped lead England to unprecedented success in the UEFA Women's European Championship, making her a record-breaking European champion.

Mead played a pivotal role in England's triumph in the European Championship, showcasing her exceptional skills, creativity, and goal-scoring ability throughout the tournament. She played as a forward, utilizing her pace, agility, and technical prowess to make a significant impact on the team's attacking play.

As the tournament progressed, Mead's performances became even more influential. She displayed her ability to create scoring opportunities for her teammates with precise passes and intelligent movement on the pitch. Her clinical finishing and composure in front of goal also saw her contribute with crucial goals for the team.

Mead's performances in the European Championship were nothing short of outstanding, earning her several individual accolades. She became the Golden Boot winner, finishing as the tournament's top goal-scorer. Additionally, her exceptional contributions earned her the title of Player of the Tournament, recognizing her as the most influential and impactful player throughout the competition. Furthermore, she topped the assist charts, showcasing her playmaking abilities and demonstrating her all-around contribution to the team's success.

England's triumph in the European Championship marked a historic moment for the team, as it was the first time they had won a major tournament. Mead's contributions were vital in achieving this milestone, and her performances will be remembered as some of the finest in the history of the competition.

Following her outstanding displays in the European Championship, Mead's achievements were widely acknowledged and celebrated. She was named as a finalist for prestigious individual awards such as the Ballon d'Or and UEFA Player of the Year, further cementing her status as one of the top players in women's football.

Mead's record-breaking European championship campaign not only showcased her immense talent but also solidified her position as a key figure in the England national team. Her contributions to the team's success will be remembered as a pivotal moment in the history of English women's football, and she will forever be recognized as an integral part of England's record-breaking European championship victory.

UEFA Women's Euro 2022

The UEFA Women's Euro 2022 was a historic tournament for Beth Mead and the England national team. Mead played a crucial role in England's success, leading them to their first-ever European championship title.

Throughout the tournament, Mead's performances were exceptional, showcasing her skill, versatility, and impact on the team's success. She played as a forward and demonstrated her ability to create scoring opportunities, both for herself and her teammates, with her vision, technical ability, and precise passing.

Mead's goal-scoring prowess was on full display as she consistently found the back of the net. Her clinical finishing and composure in front of goal played a significant role in England's success. She finished as the tournament's top goal-scorer, winning the Golden Boot, and her goals were crucial in securing victories for the team.

However, Mead's contributions were not limited to her goal-scoring ability. She also provided key assists, using her creativity and playmaking skills to set up her teammates for goals. Her ability to influence the game and create scoring opportunities made her a constant threat to opponents throughout the tournament.

In addition to her individual accolades, Mead's exceptional performances earned her the prestigious Player of the Tournament award. This recognition highlighted her impact on the tournament and her instrumental role in England's triumph.

The UEFA Women's Euro 2022 victory was a significant achievement for England, and Mead's contributions were central to their success. Her performances throughout the tournament demonstrated her ability to excel on the international stage and solidified her position as one of the top players in women's football.

Meads record-breaking performances and her role in England's historic European championship win will be remembered as a defining moment in her career and a proud moment for English women's football. Her contributions to the team's success in the UEFA Women's Euro 2022 further solidified her status as one of the finest players of her generation.

2022–23: Post-Euros acclaim

In the 2022-2023 season, Beth Mead continued to receive acclaim and recognition for her outstanding performances following England's successful UEFA Women's Euro 2022 campaign. Her post-Euros acclaim further solidified her status as one of the top players in women's football.

Mead's performances in the aftermath of the European championship showcased her consistency and continued excellence. She carried her impressive form into the domestic league, displaying her skills and playmaking abilities for her club, Arsenal, in the Women's Super League (WSL).

As the all-time leading assist provider in WSL history, Mead continued to shine as a creative force for Arsenal. Her ability to create scoring opportunities for her teammates through precise passing, intelligent movement, and accurate crosses remained a key aspect of her game. She consistently showcased her versatility and offensive prowess, playing a crucial role in Arsenal's attacking play.

Mead's performances in the 2022-2023 season garnered widespread recognition and accolades. She was named the Arsenal Player of the Season, a testament to her exceptional contributions to the team's success. This recognition highlighted her importance to Arsenal and her impact on the pitch.

Furthermore, Mead's remarkable achievements and contributions were acknowledged beyond the club level. She was named the BBC Women's Footballer of the Year, a prestigious award that recognized her as the standout player in women's football based on a public vote. This accolade reflected the admiration and support she received from fans worldwide.

In addition to her individual accolades, Mead's performances also caught the attention of the footballing world. She finished as the all-time second-highest goal contributor in WSL history, further solidifying her status as one of the league's most influential players. Her consistent goal-scoring and assist-making ability showcased her immense value to both club and country.

Mead's post-Euros acclaim highlighted her skill, talent, and impact as a player. Her recognition as the Arsenal Player of the Season and the BBC Women's Footballer of the Year, along with her impressive records in the WSL, solidified her position as one of the elite players in the women's game.

As she continued to make her mark both domestically and internationally, Mead's achievements in the 2022-2023 season served as a testament to her exceptional abilities and her status as a role model for aspiring footballers around the world.

Advocacy
Beth Mead scholarship

Beth Mead has demonstrated her commitment to supporting the next generation of athletes through her advocacy and the establishment of the Beth Mead Scholarship. In February 2022, Mead partnered with her alma mater, Teesside University, to launch the scholarship program.

The Beth Mead Scholarship aims to provide opportunities for aspiring young footballers to pursue their sporting and academic dreams. The scholarship program offers financial assistance to talented individuals who demonstrate potential in football and are seeking to further their education at Teesside University.

By establishing this scholarship, Mead seeks to give back to her community and inspire young athletes to pursue their passions. The scholarship not only recognizes the importance of academic excellence but also acknowledges the value of sports and the potential it has to transform lives.

Mead's personal journey and success serve as a testament to the power of dedication, hard work, and the support of others. Through the scholarship, she hopes to provide aspiring athletes with the resources and opportunities they need to pursue their goals, just as she was supported throughout her career.

By investing in young talents through the Beth Mead Scholarship, Mead is making a positive impact on the future of women's football and empowering individuals to reach their full potential both on and off the field. Her commitment to giving back to her community and supporting aspiring athletes showcases her dedication to the growth and development of the sport.

Women's football
ChatGPT
Women's football, also known as women's soccer, refers to the sport of football (soccer) played by women. It has gained significant popularity and recognition worldwide in recent decades, with women's football leagues, competitions, and national teams being established in many countries.

The history of women's football dates back to the late 19th century when women started playing the sport informally. However, it faced various challenges and discrimination, including restrictions, bans, and societal biases against women participating in competitive sports. Despite these obstacles, women's football gradually gained traction, and the first recorded women's football match took place in 1895 between teams representing England and Scotland.

In the modern era, women's football has experienced significant growth and development. The establishment of international tournaments such as the FIFA Women's World Cup and the UEFA Women's Euro has provided platforms for women's national teams to compete at the highest level. These tournaments have witnessed increasing levels of skill, athleticism, and competitiveness, captivating audiences and raising the profile of women's football globally.

At the club level, professional women's football leagues have been established in many countries, providing opportunities for female players to compete at a high level and pursue careers in the sport. Leagues such as the Women's Super League (WSL) in England, the National Women's Soccer League (NWSL) in the United States, and the Division 1 Feminine in France have seen significant growth in terms of popularity, investment, and competitiveness.

The visibility and recognition of women's football have been further enhanced through media coverage, sponsorships, and increased attendance at matches. Major broadcasters now dedicate airtime to women's football, and major brands have entered into partnerships and endorsement deals with female players, contributing to the commercialization and development of the sport.

Personal life
ChatGPT
Beth Mead prefers to keep her personal life private, and limited information is available about her personal life outside of football. As of my knowledge cutoff in September 2021, there have been no widely publicized details regarding her relationships, family background, or other personal aspects.

It is common for athletes, especially those in the public eye, to maintain privacy when it comes to their personal lives to focus on their careers and maintain a sense of privacy and normalcy outside of the spotlight. As a result, specific information about Beth Mead's personal life may be scarce or undisclosed.

It's important to respect athletes' privacy and recognize that they have the right to maintain boundaries between their public and personal lives. The focus is primarily on their achievements and contributions in their professional careers as athletes.

Printed in Great Britain
by Amazon

24922869R00024